Psalms for Children

Psalms for Children

Don Gordon

Illustrated by Latasha Moore

PROSPECTIVE PRESS
Winston-Salem

FAITH + KIDS

PROSPECTIVE PRESS LLC

1959 Peace Haven Rd #246, Winston-Salem, NC 27106
www.prospectivepress.com

Published in the United States of America by Prospective Press LLC

TRADEMARK

PSALMS FOR CHILDREN

ISBN 978-1-943419-26-5

This book was simultaneously published in hardcover by Prospective Press.

Printed in the United States of America
First Prospective Press printing, February, 2016

1 3 5 7 9 10 8 6 4 2

The text of this book is typeset in Adobe Minion Pro
Accent text is typeset in Adobe Jenson Pro

A version of this book was previously published under the same title
by A Pair of Docs Publishing.

Contents

Dedication

I dedicate this book
to my three wonderful daughters
and the special times we shared
reading God's Word at the end of the day.

Psalms for Children

When I was the father of three *little* girls, I used to read the Bible to them at bedtime. It was one of the favorite moments of my day, and these moments now stand as some of my most cherished memories. Because some of the words were difficult for a child to understand, I did some "on the fly" editing, changing words or phrases to something they could comprehend. The Psalms did not hold the intrigue and suspense of many of the narrative sections of the Bible, but they still held the seeds of poetry that sprouted into delight. The Psalms began to shape the concept of God these children were hiding in their hearts. When reading the Psalms, I wanted to respect the meaning of the text and use the language other translators had created, but find a way to connect with the girls I knew and loved best. Most of all, I wanted them to grow to love the Bible as I did. I hoped they would hear the majestic praises, heartfelt laments, and exhortations to righteousness that are found in the Psalms and "hide them in their hearts so they would not sin against God."

These daughters are grown and out of the house now, studying at their universities or divinity schools, and still reading in their beds at night just as I am. Now that I am having my first ever sabbatical after 27 years of ministry in local churches, I wanted to take some time to convert some of those memories into written treasures for other parents, children, and grandchildren. That's why I've created this book of Psalms with illustrations. I have extracted 25 of some of the most memorable, powerful, and child-friendly Psalms in the Bible and edited them in such a way that they will be comprehended by a child. Appreciating the diversity of the Psalms, I made an intentional effort to include all kinds of Psalms: praise, thanksgiving, lamentation, confession, wisdom, and trust. I have attempted to paraphrase these Psalms, using language and imagery appropriate for children, while remaining faithful to the spirit of these texts. Some explanatory notes along with some conversation questions are included in the back for those who might find these useful. My hope is that you will create your own special moments of reading and talking about God and the Bible with your own children, grandchildren, or any young person you love.

I am grateful to Yates Baptist Church in Durham, North Carolina for providing sabbatical time in order for me to carry out this dream. I am indebted to Dr. Andrew Wakefield, Dean of the Campbell University Divinity School (CUDS), and Irma Duke, Director of Church Relations at CUDS for providing space and hospitality at the beautiful Campbell campus, which enabled me to complete a large portion of this work. I am grateful to Dr. Tony Cartledge, Professor of Old Testament at Campbell University Divinity School for the wise counsel he provided, though I would not want to lay the burden of theological accuracy on his shoulders. I thank my wife, Elizabeth, and three daughters, Sarah, Hannah, and Rebekah, for being sources of joy and inspiration to me for more than 27 years.

I pray this book will contribute to lasting joy and a deeper love for God for all who might pick it up to read, see, and reflect on the glory and goodness of God. *Soli deo gloria.*

—Don Gordon, 2013

Psalm 1

Happy is the boy who does not hang out with the bad boys.
Happy is the girl who will not follow the girls who are mean.
Happy is the one who refuses to join in trash talk about God.

Instead he delights in the Word of God.
He reads it and thinks about it day and night.
She grows up like a big oak tree planted by a stream,
She has beautiful leaves and strong branches
That provides shade and rest for everyone.

The bad children are not like this.
They are like the dust that blows away with the slightest breeze.
Therefore, they will fall and miss out on God's blessing.

God blesses the child who does right,
But the child who constantly does wrong will be ruined.

Psalm 8

O Lord, our God,

> How awesome is your name in all the world!
> Your glory goes way beyond the stars!

From the lips of babies and toddlers praise rings out,
Drowning out the voices of your enemies and non-believers.

When I look into the heavens at nighttime
And see the work of your fingers—
The moon and stars and planets that you set in orbit,
I wonder, "Who am I, little ol' me?
What makes you think about me God?
Why do you love and care for me so much?"

Yet you have crowned me with glory and honor,
Put me in charge of your creation,
All the birds in the sky,
All the sheep, cows, and horses,
All the fish in the sea and the ponds,
Everything on earth is under my care!
Wow!

O Lord, Our God,

> How awesome is your name in all the world.

Psalm 15

Lord, who gets invited to your house?
    Who gets to live with you in your home?

The one who lives the right way,
    Does the right things,
    Speaks the truth;

The one who doesn't hurt his friend,
    Never spreads bad gossip about his buddy,
    Despises the evil he sees,
    And honors those who serve God;

The one who keeps his word even when it costs,
    Lends money to a friend in time of need
    And does not take a bribe.

Those who do these things will be invited to the house of God
And live in security and peace forever.

Psalm 19

The heavens tell a powerful story of God's glory;
    The skies shout a song about the work of God's hands.
Each day announces a new word;
    Every night another story is told.
No matter what language people speak
    They can hear and understand these lessons.
The voice of God, speaking through the heavens,
    Is heard from one corner of the world to another.

In the heavens God has cast the sun onto a canvas,
Surrounded with orbiting planets and distant stars.
The sun comes up in the morning
Like a powerful runner coming over a hill,
Never resting and never tiring.
No one can miss the light and heat coming from his heels.

Psalm 23

The Lord is my shepherd,
I have everything I need.

He takes me to fields of soft, green grass.
He leads me to running creeks with cool water.
He lets me play and rest so I can grow strong.
He shows me the right path to take so I won't get in trouble.

Even when I have to walk through the valley of death,
I won't be afraid, God, for you are with me.
Your shepherd's staff makes me feel safe.

You prepare a huge feast for me
    Right in front of my enemies.
You strengthen my spirits and give me fresh energy;
    I have more than I can possibly use.

I know your goodness and love will follow me
    All the days of my life;
And I will dwell in the house of the Lord forever.

Psalm 46

God is our fortress where we can hide when we are in trouble or afraid.
Therefore, we will not fear even if
    Hurricanes come to the coast,
    Tornadoes sweep across the plains, and
    Earthquakes shake the mountains.

There is a place where God lives,
    A crystal clear river runs through it bringing joy
    To God and everyone who lives there.
That city is safe; it can never be taken over by enemies;
    God would never allow it.
Nations wage war, kingdoms fall,
But when God speaks,
The nations are silenced,
    Kingdoms bow down,
    The earth trembles at the sound of his voice.

The Lord Almighty is with us; the God of Jacob is our fortress.

Come and see all the amazing things God has done,
    No tree has grown to the sky or fallen to the ground
Without his knowledge.
    He makes wars end,
    He destroys guns, missiles, and bombs,

Heaping them into a pile of harmless junk.
Be quiet. Be still. Know that I am God.
    I am over the nations.
    I am the creator of the earth.

The Lord Almighty is with us; the God of Jacob is our fortress.

Psalm 51

Please God, have mercy on me.
Show me your love, offer me compassion, and erase away my sins.
Clean me inside and out.

I know what my sins are. Even when I try not to think about them
They are right there in my mind.
It's you I have sinned against, disobeying you and you alone.
Yes, you are right to judge me and discipline me.
I have been sinful since I was in my mother's womb.

But you want integrity, honesty, and truthfulness.
So cleanse me, make me as white as snow.
Put joy in my life again and a song in my heart.
Let me dance in the knowledge of my forgiveness.
God, give me a new start and a clean heart today.
Don't ever leave me or take your Spirit from me.
Make me happy again with the knowledge of your salvation.
Bend my will towards yours today and always.

Psalm 84

How lovely is the house of God, the God who rules over all.

I can't wait to go there to worship you with the people of God.

Every part of me wants to sing praises to God,

And feel the Living God in my heart and soul.

Even the birds want to sing their songs in the house of God.

They want to build a nest somewhere, anywhere in the sanctuary

So they can hatch their eggs, feed their young,

And chirp songs of praise to the Lord God Almighty.

How blessed are those who dwell in your house,

Praising your name day and night.

How blessed are those who depend on you for strength,

Who walk with you down the roads of their life.

When they reach dry valleys you will fill it with cool springs

And drench the ground with rain.

They will find you at the end of their journey.

What joy will be theirs.

Listen to me God. I'm praying to you.

God of Jacob, you have chosen me. Give me your blessing.

Spending one day in your house is better than a thousand days elsewhere.

I would rather sweep the floor in your house than hang out with the wicked.

For the Lord God is my light and protector;

The Lord offers grace and honor,

He withholds nothing the children who follow him.

O Lord, ruler of all, blessed is the child who trusts in you.

Psalm 90

Lord, before you knew me you knew my parents and grandparents.
You go back with my family for longer than I can count.
Before the mountains jutted up from the earth, you were there.
Before one blade of grass grew out of the ground, you were there.

Time is nothing to you. A thousand years to you is like a day to my family.
We came from dust, and to dust we will return.
Please don't stay angry at us for our sins.
We couldn't go on if we knew you would stay angry forever.
We only live 70 years, 80 if our heart stays strong.
Trouble and sadness come to everybody soon enough.
So teach us to appreciate how precious every single day is.
Give us wisdom to live smarter and more obediently in all our tomorrows.

Bless us Lord, so that our lives matter and make a difference in the world.
Work through our hands to fulfill your divine purposes.

Psalm 91

The children who find their safety and security in God can say this:
"God, I am always safe around you.
    That's why I trust you."

For God will protect you from all forms of evil;
Everyone who tries to harm you will fail.
Like a mother eagle covers her offspring,
God will cover you with his wings.

When night time comes there's no need to be afraid.
When day comes you can play in safety.
Others may be harmed when they oppose God,
But you will be safe because God is your guide and protector.
His angels will watch over you; you won't even stump your toe.

God says to you, "Because I love you I will protect you.
When you call my name I will answer.
I will save you when you get into trouble.
Through my power you will grow up and grow old,
Basking in the salvation that comes from me."

Psalm 93

The Lord is king, wearing a beautiful robe,
    Standing tall and walking strong.

He made the world and all things in it;
    It will never fall apart.

The Lord has been on his throne a long time;
    Before anything else existed, the Lord was on his throne.

Look, the waves of the ocean are rushing in,
The waves are crashing on the sand,
The waves are roaring with a loud voice.

Stronger than the roaring of the waves,
Mightier than crash of waves on the seashore,
The Lord laughs and tells the waves what to do.

Your laws, O God, are steady and firm.
Your home is decorated with holiness.
It always has been and always will be.

Psalm 98

Sing to the Lord a new song,
For he has done amazing things.
He rolled up his sleeves and got the job done;
He brought salvation to people around the world,
And showed them his righteousness.

He remembered his love for his people, Israel,
A love that will never fail.

Shout for joy to the Lord, everyone shout loud.
Sing happy songs, write new songs about the Lord;
Play the piano, blow the trumpet, dance with grace
Before the Lord who listens from his throne.

Let the sea and all the fish in the ocean join in the singing,
Let the rivers claps their hands,
Let the mountains rock to the rhythm.
Let them all join in the singing for the Lord,
    Who judges what is right and wrong.
He will make the right judgments and be fair to everyone.

Psalm 100

Make a joyful noise to the Lord, everyone on earth.

Come to worship the Lord with glad singing.

Know that the Lord is God.

He made us and we are his children.

We are his people and he will take care of us.

Enter his house of worship with thankful hearts,

Enter into his presence with praise.

Say, "Thank you Lord, blessings to you."

For the Lord is good,

His love for you lasts forever,

From generation to generation, his love never runs out.

Psalm 103

Praise the Lord, body and soul!
From my head to my toe, I praise his holy name.
I will not forget all that he has done for me:

He forgives my sin,

He heals my body,

He saves me for eternity,

He surrounds me with love,

He gives me life day after day,

He sets things right.

Long ago he did this for Moses and the people of God.

The Lord treats me better than I deserve.
It takes a long time for him to get angry,
Even then, he never stops loving me.
He gets over his anger and does not punish me the way I deserve.

His love for me reaches higher than the stars in the sky.
He takes my sins far across the mountains and past the oceans,
Burying them so they can never be found.
He is like a father who has compassion for his children,
Like a mother who remembers the day they were born.

Compared to the everlasting love of God,
My life is like grass that turns green in spring and brown in the fall.
But God is eternal, his love his everlasting,
And those who respect him will never be abandoned by him.

The Lord rules over heaven and earth;
He is the king of every nation.

So bless God, angels who serve him.
Bless God, servants who obey him.
Bless God, creatures far and wide who point to him.
Bless God, me, from my head to my toe, bless God.

Psalm 104

Praise the Lord, body and soul!

How awesome you are.
You make the heavens your home,
You ride the clouds around like big puffy cars.
You made the world with it deep oceans
      Tall mountains
      Grassy plains
      Running streams
      Powerful lions
      Fast horses
      Sweet peach trees
      Growing families
Everyone and everything looks to you for life.
Like a baby chick awaits food from its mother so we wait on you.
If we don't find you we are scared for we depend on you.
Everything depends on you.

It will always be like this, your power never fades away.
So I will sing to you all my life.
May you be pleased with my songs and prayers,
For it pleases me to please you, O God.

Praise the Lord, body and soul.

Psalm 111

Praise the Lord!

A round of applause for God from my heart.

Back me up, you people of God.

Count how many great things God has done.

Delight in his goodness my friends.

Earth sings of his glory and majesty.

Forever is he faithful.

Great wonders will always be remembered.

His mercy and grace are matchless.

In him we receive daily bread.

Joy comes from knowing he keeps his promises.

Kneel down before the all-powerful God.

Land is ours because it is a gift from the Lord.

Mighty are the works of his hands.

Never are his laws unfair.

Only God's laws last forever.

Pay attention and you'll see how faithful God is.

Quit searching for salvation outside God.

Remember his promises made to Israel.

See how awesome and holy our God is.

Trust in the Lord is the beginning of wisdom.

Understanding comes from following his laws.

Virtue clothes him and therefore I will praise him.

Wait on the Lord and you will be blessed. (112:1a)

X-ray vision discovers the joy of his commands. (112:1b)

You will be great in the land if you serve God. (112:2a)

Zealous generations will be blessed by God. (112:2b)

Psalm 119

I am happy because I live according to the Law of God.

I am blessed because I keep the Law and love God with all my heart.

In my heart I store up your words so I will not sin against you.

Teach me your commands, O God, and I will obey them the rest of my life.

The bullies may make fun of me, but I will not turn away from your words.

Oh how I love your law! I think about it all day long.

Your word is a flashlight so I won't stumble or lose my way

>   On the path of doing right.

I become very sad when I see that your Law is not obeyed.

Your words are absolutely true; your laws are eternal.

Psalm 121

When I look up to the mountains I ask,
"Where can I go for help?"
And then my answer comes, "Your help comes from the Lord,
    The creator of heaven and earth."

God will not let me slip and fall;
God is always paying attention to me, he never sleeps.
In fact, he pays attention to all his children.
He never sleeps, nor does he take a nap.

God protects me;
When it's too hot he covers me with shade.
God won't let me burn from the sun during the day,
Nor let moon scare me at night.

God keeps me safe from all evil;
He protects my life.
He keeps me safe when I leave home in the morning
    And when I return in the evening.
God will be my protector now and forever.

Psalm 131

Lord, I'm not walking around thinking I'm better than everybody else.
I don't look down on other people.
I'm not trying to become famous.

I'm happy being me, sitting quietly in your presence.
I know I'm just a kid and I'm fine with that.
In fact, I like being a kid who trusts you for everything.

I think everyone would be better off if they thought like that.
People of God, put your hope in the Lord and not in yourself.

Psalm 136

Give thanks to the Lord, for he is good.
> His love lives on forever.

He has done amazing wonders.
> His love lives on forever.

Only God had the mind and imagination to create the world.
> His love lives on forever.

He spoke a word and creation began.
> His love lives on forever.

He spoke the planets and stars into the sky.
> His love lives on forever.

He chose a people to be his special family.
> His loves lives on forever.

He rescued them from slavery in Egypt.
> His love lives on forever.

He brought them out of Egypt and to the Red Sea.
> His love lives on forever.

He opened the Red Sea for them so they could escape.
> His loves lives on forever.

He led his people through the desert.
> His loves lives on forever.

He brought them to the Promised Land.
> His love lives on forever.

He gave his people the land as a special gift.
> His love lives on forever.

He remembered them when they were lowly and saved them.
> His love lives on forever.

God frees us from our enemies.
> His loves lives on forever.

God gives food to people and animal.
> His loves lives on forever.

Give thanks to God for his amazing wonders.
> His love lives on forever.

Psalm 139

God, you know my mind and heart better than anyone;
    You know me better than I know myself.
You know when I sit down and when I get up;
    You know what I'm thinking.
You know where I have gone and where I'm going.
God, you know every single word I say before I say it.
You go ahead of me and stand behind me.
You place your hand on me and bless me.
This is awesome, too wonderful for me to take in.

Is there anywhere I can go where you aren't already there?
If I go into outer space, you are there.
If I die, you will be there more me.
If I move to another city or another country, you will be there too.
Wherever I go, you will be with me.
If I get lost and it becomes night time, you will know where I am.
    You are never in the dark.

For you created me, and placed me in my mother's womb.
I praise you because I am like your own special work of art—
    Beautiful and wonderful.
    I know that is true.
When I was growing inside my mother you could see me.
You watched my hands form, my legs grow, my eyes twinkle.
All my days ahead in my life you knew ahead of time.
How awesome is your mind, how great are your thoughts.
You have more thoughts than grains of sand on all the beaches in the world.
Who can count that high?

Search me, O God, and know my heart.
Test me, all my thoughts and deeds.
If there is anything I have thought or done that is wrong,
    Show me so I can walk the right road with you all my days.

Psalm 142

O God, I cry out to you today.

I beg you for help.

I bring you my troubles; I tell you my complaints.

When I'm at my lowest point,

     You are the one who knows how bad it is.

During the day bad people are trying to hurt me.

If you look around, you'll see no one is coming to help me.

I have no place to go, no one seems to care.

So I cry to you, O God;

I say, "You are my safety, you are the only hope I have."

Listen to me God; I'm desperate.

Save me from those who are trying to hurt me.

Help me find an escape, and I will tell everyone you did.

Your people will surround me with protection,

Because they see how good you really are.

Psalm 146

Praise the Lord!
Praise the Lord, O my soul!
I will praise the Lord all the days of my life.

Do not trust in presidents and governors.
They are just people who can't give you salvation.
They die like all people, and their great plans die with them.

Blessed is the one whose help is in the Lord,
    Whose hope is in God,
    The maker of heaven and earth,
    The fish of the sea
    The birds of the air
    The animals on the ground.
The Lord will never let you down.

He defends the poor and gives food to the hungry.
He frees prisoners and gives sight to the blind.
He encourages those who are burdened and loves those who do right.
He cares for the immigrant,
He loves the orphan,
He protects the widow.
He opposes those who are wicked.

The Lord is in charge now and forever.
Praise the Lord.

Psalm 149

Praise the Lord!
Sing to the Lord a new song.
Gather the choir and sing together in church.

Let the people of God sing their joy;
Praise the Lord with dancing and making music with instruments.
For the Lord loves when his people worship with joy;
Humble, child-like worship makes God smile.
Everyone worship with joy wherever you are—at church or at home.

May the worship of God bring about the judgment against evil,
So that wicked nations and cruel people will be punished,
Their leaders put in prison and getting what they deserve.
This is all for the glory of God.
Praise the Lord!

Psalm 150

Praise the Lord!
Praise God in his sanctuary.
Praise him in the sky above.
Praise him for all the mighty things he has done.
Praise him for being the greatest of the great.
Praise him with the trumpet and trombone.
Praise him with the cello and violin.
Praise him with drums and dancing.
Praise him with the guitar and mandolin.
Praise him with loud cymbals and a bass drum.
Let everything that breathes praise the Lord.
Praise the Lord!

Appendix A
A Description of the Psalms

1 . . . . Wisdom Psalm

8 . . . . Praise Psalm

15 . . . . Worship Entry Psalm

19 . . . . Creation Psalm

23 . . . . Trust Psalm

46 . . . . Song of Zion

51 . . . . Song of Penitence

84 . . . . Song of Zion

90 . . . . Community Lament

91 . . . . Song of Protection

93 . . . . Enthronement Psalm

98 . . . . Enthronement Psalm

100 . . . . Song of Thanksgiving

103 . . . . Song of Praise

104 . . . . Creation Psalm

111/112 . . . . Acrostic Praise

119 . . . . Acrostic Torah Psalm

121 . . . . Song of Trust

131 . . . . Song of Child-Like Trust

136 . . . . Song of Thanksgiving

139 . . . . Song of God's Knowledge

142 . . . . Psalm of Lament

147 . . . . Hallelujah Song

149 . . . . New Song

150 . . . . Musical Praise Psalm

Appendix B
Notes and Conversation Questions

Psalm 1

Questions: Do other children ever try to get you to do bad things? How do you handle that?

Psalm 8

Notes: Go outside at night, lie down on a blanket, and gaze. Then read the Psalm and gaze into the sky.

You could also talk about what it means that we are in charge of creation, to be stewards of this earth.

Psalm 15

Notes: This Psalm addresses ethical issues for the people of God and the expectations God has for their behavior. Pick any of the phrases in this litany and discuss them with your child.

Psalm 19

Question: What do you believe the sky is telling you today/tonight?

Psalm 23

Notes: This would be a good Psalm to read at a picnic. It could be used to help prompt a discussion after the death of a loved one. The point in both instances is God's provision for us in happy and sad times.

Psalm 46

Notes: This could be a good Psalm to read when your child is hearing about war or violence. It could be used to encourage quiet times with God. It may prompt a lesson about who Jacob is (Gen 25-37).

Psalm 51

Question: How do you feel after you have confessed to God something you have done wrong?

Psalm 84

Question: What do you like about going to church?

Psalm 90

Notes: This is an opportunity to talk about the faith of older people, even those people the child may never have met. This will help your child see that faith in God continues generation to generation.

Psalm 91

Question: What makes you feel safe?

Psalm 93

Notes: This could be a good Psalm to read at the beach or ocean. You can talk about God controlling the waves.
Question: What does the ocean sound like to you? How does it make you feel to listen to the waves?

Psalm 98

Notes: Let this be a Psalm to prompt the singing or teaching of a new song.

Psalm 100

Question: What has God done good for you? How do you think God feels when we sing praises to him and worship him?

Psalm 103

Question: What do you think it means that "the Lord treats me better than I deserve?"
How does it make you feel that God carries your sin away so far that it will never bother you again?

Psalm 104

Notes: This Psalm could prompt a conversation about the vastness and diversity of God's creation.

Psalm 111

Notes: This is an acrostic Psalm in which every half verse began with a successive letter of the Hebrew alphabet. Psalm 112 is also an acrostic Psalm. Since the English alphabet has four more letters than the Hebrew alphabet, I have added the first four verses of Psalm 112 to this Psalm.

Psalm 119

Notes: This longest Psalm in the Bible has been abbreviated using some of the most memorable verses of this creative poem highlighting the beauty of God's Law.
Question: What is so wonderful about God's laws and commands?

Psalm 121

Notes: This would be a good Psalm to read at the mountains or after taking a hike up a mountain.

Psalm 131

Question: What do you like about you? (This can be an opportunity to affirm the uniqueness of your child).

Psalm 136

Notes: This would be a good Psalm to read together with one person reading the verse and the other reading the chorus "His love lives on forever."
Notes: Some of the violent verses of the original Psalm have been skipped for child developmental purposes.

Psalm 139

Question: Did you know that God knew you before you were born? How does that make you feel?
Notes: This Psalm could be used as part of a conversation about the interdependence of the divine and human in the procreative process.

Psalm 142

Notes: This Psalm of Lament can be a prompt to a conversation about bullies and people trying to hurt others. Depending on God can be a confidence builder for children rather than an escape.

Question: Do other people try to hurt you? What do you do?

Psalm 146

Notes: This Psalm can serve to show how God cares for different groups of people who suffer. Use this Psalm to bring these groups to mind and encourage a sympathetic heart towards them.

Psalm 149

Question: What are your favorite songs to sing at church?

Psalm 150

Question: What kind of musical instruments do you like to play? Do you like to listen to?

Notes: Talk about all kinds of musical instruments being used to praise God.

About the Author

DON GORDON has served as the pastor of Ardmore Baptist Church in Winston-Salem, North Carolina since 2013. Prior to that, he served as a pastor at churches in Durham, Mount Olive, and Spruce Pine, North Carolina; and Emporia, Virginia. He and his wife Elizabeth have been married since 1985 and have three daughters: Sarah, Hannah, and Rebekah.

He earned a Doctorate of Ministry degree from Columbia Theological Seminary (PCUSA), an M.Div. from Southeastern Baptist Theological Seminary, and a B.S. degree in Mathematics from Campbell University, where he was a four-year lettermen in tennis. He did further graduate studies in Mathematics at N.C. State University. Currently he is serving on the Board of Trustees for Campbell University and the Board of Directors for The Baptist Center for Ethics in Nashville, Tennessee.

Don's first book, *Like Drops of Morning Dew: A Concise History of North Carolina Baptists*, was published by the Baptist State Convention of North Carolina and distributed to its 3,800 churches. *Psalms for Children* is Don's second book. Having sold out its initial paperback print run and seeing the closure of its original publisher, *Psalms* has been picked up and republished by Prospective Press, in both trade paperback and hardcover.

An ACC basketball fan for life, Don enjoys playing, watching, and coaching a number of sports, particularly basketball and tennis.

CPSIA information can be obtained at www.ICGtesting.com
Printed in the USA
BVOW07s2100080216

436020BV00003B/4/P